HELLO FAILURE

KRISTEN KOSMAS

EMERGENCY PLAYSCRIPTS
UGLY DUCKLING PRESSE
BROOKLYN, NY

HELLO FAILURE
COPYRIGHT KRISTEN KOSMAS, 2009

EMERGENCY PLAYSCRIPTS #1

ISBN 978-1-933254-56-2

SERIES EDITORS
THE BROS. LUMIÈRE

FIRST EDITION, 2009
UGLY DUCKLING PRESSE
232 THIRD STREET, E002
BROOKLYN, NY 11215
>WWW.UGLYDUCKLINGPRESSE.ORG<

CATALOGING-IN-PUBLICATION DATA
AVAILABLE FROM
THE LIBRARY OF CONGRESS

FUNDED IN PART BY
THE NATIONAL ENDOWMENT
FOR THE ARTS

DISTRIBUTED BY
SMALL PRESS DISTRIBUTION
1341 SEVENTH STREET
BERKELEY, CA 94710
>WWW.SPDBOOKS.ORG<

PRINTED IN THE USA

HELLO FAILURE

KRISTEN KOSMAS

HELLO FAILURE was first presented as a workshop, directed by the playwright, at Dixon Place in May, 2005.

It was presented again as a staged reading in the PRELUDE.07 Festival, directed by Ken Rus Schmoll.

In March, 2008, it premiered at Performance Space 122, directed by Ken Rus Schmoll, with the following cast: Michael Chick, Benjamin Forster, Janna Gjesdal, Megan Hart, Joan Jubett, Kristen Kosmas, Matthew Maher, Aimee Phelan-Deconinck, Tricia Rodley, and Maria Striar.

The playwright would like to thank the following actors who worked on the play in its developmental stages: Hannah Cabell, Jena Cane, Chris Caniglia, Peter Carrs, Alissa Ford, Ki Gottberg, Stephen Hando, Sarah Harlett, Elizabeth Kenny, Shannon Kipp, Denver Latimer, Annie McNamara, Sean Nelson, Chara Riegel, Tina Rowley, Kate Ryan, Heidi Schreck, Jenny Schwartz, Mike Shapiro, Valerie Trucchia, and Juliette Waller.

Additional very special thanks to Andy Horwitz, and to James Copeland.

Funding for this edition was provided in part by the National Endowment for the Arts.

NATIONAL ENDOWMENT FOR THE ARTS

CHARACTERS
(IN ORDER OF SPEAKING)

Horace Hunley
Netta
Kate
Rebecca
Shlomy
Gina
Valeska
The Japanese
Karen
The New Girl, Margerie
Tim

THE PLAY takes place in the present.

On stage, there is a coffee urn and a
large potted plant that I know of.

When the characters speak on cell
phones, consider the absence of actual
cell phones. Consider the absence of
flowers, of the bed.

(For further production considerations,
see author's notes at the end of the
script.)

NOTE
The appearance of two slash marks
(//) in the middle of a line indicates that
the next character's line begins at that
point.

PROLOGUE

SUBMARINE SOUNDS IN THE DARK.

HORACE: The concept of a boat
that would sail underwater

NETTA: *(LOUD, LIKE TO AN AUDITORIUM)* H L Hun—

HORACE: dates back as far as the sixteenth century.

NETTA: *(TRYING AGAIN)* Horace L Hunl—

HORACE: That's the fifteen hundreds. If you can imagine.

NETTA: *(AGAIN)* Horace—
Ah gahd. I don't think I can do this today.

NETTA EXITS.

HORACE: The submersible boat was not invented by a single person but was, rather, developed, in many slow, and as it proved sometimes, painful steps.

NETTA: *(RE-ENTERING, LOUD)* Horace Lawson Hunley was a marine engineer during the American Civil War who developed early, hand-powered submarines, the most famous of which, the H L Hunley, was the first submarine in the history of naval warfare to attack and sink a ship. Unfortunately, shortly after the attack, the Hunley sank, for the fourth time, and everyone on board died, *(FADING OUT)* and the boat was lost for more than 130 years until it was…

KATE: Do you like to ride horses?

REBECCA: Dear Jack, I am standing in this abstract and unnecessary river.

KATE: Do you like to fly kites?

REBECCA: It feels so life-like, so much like real.

KATE: Can you fly an airplane, do you know who invented the airplane?

SHLOMY: The Wright Brothers?

KATE: Yes! Yes I think that's it! Yes … I think so too.

SHLOMY: I had a brother once, wanted to fly.

GINA: *(ON THE PHONE WITH NETTA, TALKING ABOUT HER KID)* Mommy what is that? Mommy what are those? Mommy what are you? Mommy what am I? Mommy what are these? What is this, are those knives, is that a book, is this myself Mommy, are you a man?

NETTA: You want to know what he said? First thing when he came home? When he walked into the bedroom he said, That penny was there in the exact same place when I left. That penny was there on the floor in the exact same place when I left. And I said, Well why didn't you pick it up? And he said, Why didn't you pick it up? And I said, Why didn't you drown? And he said, Nice Netta. Real nice.

VALESKA: We all just. TALK. So much. Couldn't we just—And do we really SAY ANYTHING? I mean. What are we saying? Couldn't we just. Be quiet? For a minute just. Be quiet? And listen?

THE
JAPANESE: We don't have the article in the same way as you do. That will take some getting used to. Nor the gender nor the quantity neither. We don't care so much how about how many of them there are. Nor do we care if they are masculine or feminine. We think you can figure that out for yourself. Based on the context. We leave that up to your intelligence. Which is, I think, somewhat different from your language. I think, in your language, this is not the case.

KAREN: I think that's true. I think it is different in my language. I don't think there is so much left up to the intelligence.

NEW GIRL: *(ON THE PHONE TO KATE)* Down at the Holy Name of Jesus School, past Robert DeNiro and the snowflakes, and the fire hydrant and the politics, a miniature laundress will pass you by. Panamanian. She'll be Panamanian. And then the bucket and the ladder, and an interracial couple, and just a few more steps and—maybe half a block and—it's Paradise. Paradise Dry Cleaners. Then, Our Lady Mary Baseball Diamond, and the drive-through window where you get the stained glass while the white stockings and the nurse's shoes squeak by and the flower pots crash down on your head, and then a little boy, or a girl, someone small says, I wanna go down there to the rainbow. And then an adult, a man says, Not by yourself. You can't go down there alone. Only with one of the two of us. But there is only one of them. Today. Only him, so it seems: no rainbow. Is the answer. Is that today, there will be no rainbow. And that's how you'll know you're close. After that, we're the second house on the left. Top bell.

AN ALARM CLOCK GOES OFF. AND OFF. AND OFF.

REBECCA: I can't. Today. Not today I don't think I can. Maybe not ever again.

ALARM CLOCK OUT.

VALESKA: Couldn't we all just—listen for a minute and be quiet and just—be quiet and listen?

REBECCA: Dear Horace Hunley,
I don't know where to send this letter. I don't know if you are in heaven or hell right now so I don't know if you are getting this but—

While on the one hand, I don't think that there is anyone like me anywhere else in this whole wide world—I think on the other hand, Horace, that you and I have something in common. Which is how we both started out with such promise.

I know you had a terrible falling out with my mother many years ago, but I hope that didn't change your feelings for me, Horace, which if I remember correctly were basically fond. Yes, I think you had a tenderness for me, Horace Hunley, in spite of everything, which I appreciated even then, and so, if you're available, I would sure love it if you could come by.

I'm in my bathroom. On the floor. Which is where you'll find me.

Signed,
Your nephew,
Roger.

BLACKOUT.

REBECCA: I'm just kidding.

LIGHTS UP.

REBECCA: Sincerely,
Rebecca.
Rebecca.
Rebecca.

NETTA: You know in all that stuff they give us, all the literature, everything they say about the—Stages of Deployment and all of the—corresponding emotional feelings and all of the—stupidass activities they suggest? I don't find sometimes that they give me one useful bit of goddamn information. Sometimes I feel like I just wanna—drive my car off the bridge or—eat a whole goddamn cake you know? You know what I'm saying? You know what I'm saying?

GINA: I do. Actually. I do know what you're saying.
I ate a whole goddamn cake last night.

VALESKA: Stop it! I'm serious! Stop it! Just—shut up! For one minute! Just stop—talking. For one minute. All right? All right?

REBECCA: Or you could call me on the phone! I have that in here too. I sleep in here sometimes. In the bathtub when I'm—Our house is too big Horace. Jack says I'm the only wife on the Eastern Seaboard who complains that her house is too big. I say OK. I'm the only wife on the Eastern Seaboard who complains that her house is too big. So what? If we'd had that baby maybe— But something is wrong with my insides Horace. Did you ever know that? Did my mother ever tell you that? You probably don't like to talk about that stuff though. Most men don't. Most people don't. I don't.

THE
JAPANESE: So we don't care so much about men and man, or knives and knife. But we are interested in these and those, this and that.

KAREN: And what is the difference between those things?

VALESKA
& THE
JAPANESE: It has to do with nearness. Proximity. This—is close to you, while that—is further away.

KAREN: Ah OK, yes, mm hm, I see that.

SCENE ONE

NETTA STANDS IN THE MIDDLE OF AN EMPTY CONFERENCE ROOM AT THE SUBMARINE MUSEUM WHERE SHE WORKS. FLUORESCENT LIGHTS. ROOM TONE FOR A LONG TIME. SHE STARES INTO SPACE FOR A FEW SECONDS. THEN SHE CALLS OFF-STAGE TO TIM.

NETTA: Hey? Tim?

TIM: Yeah?

NETTA: Yeah, hey, can we get a couple of conference tables brought into the—

TIM: Conference room?

NETTA: Right. Right yeah at ten?

TIM: Yeah at ten.

NETTA: OK.

TIM: OK.

NETTA: OK thanks.

SCENE TWO

*KATE AND SHLOMY APPEAR. THEY ARE IN BED
TOGETHER, NAKED, LANGUORING, SMILING.*

KATE: Do you like to climb trees? Are you good at that? There is a tree that I would like to climb. It's gigantic and looks soft. Safe. It's outside my window. I would just like to climb out there and crawl up there and nestle into a crook in one of its branches, and rest my head in the leaves up there and just lie there, in the air, and the clouds, and the weather.

SHLOMY: You like to talk about the weather?

KATE: I don't mind it. I like to talk about anything.

LANGUOR.

SHLOMY: I used to want to be a scientist.

KATE: Are you serious?

SHLOMY: Yes. I am. What? I went to college.

KATE: Really?

SHLOMY: Yes, really. What, you think because I'm a hairdresser I'm not educated?

KATE: I don't know, well. Yes, it does come as a bit of a surprise. But actually, now that you're saying it, maybe I would have known it if I'd given it any thought.

SHLOMY: You don't give me any thought?

KATE: That's not what I meant.

SMILE.

SHLOMY: I had a brother once. Wanted to fly. Thought he could fly. Was the most heartbreaking thing you ever laid eyes on. Wings flapping around like that. Feathers flying off his arms. Horrible. Beautiful. Terrible. Fantastic.

KATE: Did he die?

SHLOMY: He did. He died. He did.

KATE: In a flying accident?

SHLOMY: No. Not exactly. No. Not exactly.

KATE: I'm sorry.

SHLOMY: That's OK. It was a long time ago.

AN ALARM CLOCK GOES OFF.

KATE: Nooo! I don't think I can. Not today. Maybe not ever again.

SHLOMY: Don't go. Don't go if you don't want to.

KATE: I have to. I'm picking up the new girl.

SCENE THREE

GINA AND NETTA IN THE CONFERENCE ROOM.

NETTA: So I think we have a new girl coming in today.

GINA: Really? A new girl? That's great.

NETTA: Yeah so I just want everything to be nice for her you know. I just want everything to be kinda just right.

NETTA EXITS TO GET SOMETHING OR DO SOMETHING.

KATE: I don't know, Shlomy. I don't think there is anyone like me anywhere else in this whole godforsaken world.

SHLOMY: … Neither do I.

KATE AND SHLOMY DISAPPEAR.

VALESKA: *(ENTERING THE CONFERENCE ROOM)* Hello!

GINA: Hi Valeska.

VALESKA: Hi Gina how are you?

GINA: I'm good I'm OK how are you?

VALESKA: I'm fine. I brought some flowers.

NETTA: *(COMING BACK IN)* Oh good! Because we have a new girl coming in today and so I want everything to be nice for her you know?

VALESKA: Of course. Where should I put them?

NETTA: Just anywhere's fine.

VALESKA: It's good that the weather has changed, no?

NETTA: Yes. Yes it is good. The weather helps.

GINA: *(TO NETTA)* Or not...

NETTA: No it does it helps it's good.

VALESKA: But I think that the weather is always beautiful, I don't
             know.

NETTA: *(TO VALESKA)* You want some coffee?

GINA: Always? Even last week?

VALESKA: No that's OK I had some already, but yes, even last
             week, but I think that all of the kinds of weather are
             beautiful. It is only ourselves that get into bad moods
             about it. But the weather itself? If you take it for how it
             is? It's not personal. And there's always something to
             see good in it. Its particular qualities. Each kind. It can
             wake you up. It is always something that is available to
             you to experience.

KAREN: *(ENTERING)* Are we talking about the weather again?

VALESKA: Why not? It's lovely.

KAREN: Today it is. Last week it wasn't so good.

GINA: No apparently that was only you. That was only you
             that wasn't so good last week.

KAREN: Can I get some coffee?

GINA: Yeah I think it's ready.

GINA GETS KAREN A CUP OF COFFEE.

NETTA: The only kind of weather I really don't like is smog.
             When it's hazy.

VALESKA: But that isn't weather is it? Smog? That's just pollution.
             That is something on top of the weather no? It isn't the
             weather itself is it?

NETTA: Well anyway I don't like it.

VALESKA: OK.

KAREN: What time is it?

GINA: It's ten.

KAREN: Where is everybody? I thought I was running late. Where's Kate? Where's Rebecca?

NETTA: I think Kate is bringing the New Girl and ... I don't know where Rebecca is.

GINA'S CELL PHONE RINGS.

KAREN: The new girl? There's a new girl coming today?

GINA: I'm sorry excuse me you guys.

NETTA: Yeah.

GINA: Hello?

KAREN: That's nice.

GINA: Yes.

NETTA: I know I think so too.

GINA: Unh-hunh yes I did that's right.

            No. No I didn't.

            No I told him only that he wouldn't have any rest until he admitted what a colossal disaster it was.

            Well that is the job of my department.

            I know he doesn't want to think of it like that, but those are the facts.

            No, I don't know his name.

No, I didn't call him by his name, that's true.

But I didn't think I was supposed to call him by his name, I didn't think I was supposed to get involved like that.

I thought that was why we numbered the cases by case number. That was your idea, not mine.

You told me to follow it. You told me to follow his case because you thought his proposition was risky.

No but isn't that my job? To be skeptical?

Well I'm sorry he feels that way but—

OK but he put the careers of thirty of his co-workers on the line for the sake of his project which was an absolute catastrophe and now all of their lives are ruined.

Yes all of them! Don't you read the papers? You publish them, you really should read them.

No, yes, their lives are ruined. Yes all of them! So who's really the bad guy here I mean me? Or him?

Well I don't think really it's me if you think about it.

Uhm ... if you think about it I think you'll have to—

OK well I disagree.
OK well then we'll just have to agree to disagree.

Oh that's a—
That's ridiculous! I'm going to have to call you back.
No, I'm going to call you back. I'll call you back!

Gahd! They hire me to do this shitty job that no one else wants because no one else can handle it because they're a bunch of fuckin sissies, and then they get all upset when I actually do it. // Ulgh. Whatever.

NETTA: I really wish you wouldn't swear. Gina. I wish you wouldn't do that.

GINA: Sorry.

NETTA: It's OK.

GINA: Do we have any—Do we have any like—

NETTA: What?

GINA: I don't know, something to chew on?

KAREN: You mean like gum?

GINA: No. Forget it.

NETTA: You want a straw? A coffee stirrer?

GINA: All right. Yeah. Yeah give me one of those.

> *NETTA GIVES HER A COFFEE STIRRER.*
> *SHE CHEWS ON IT. BEAT. BEAT.*

KAREN: How's your job going?

VALESKA: OK. I told the children to shut up yesterday.

KAREN: You did?

VALESKA: Yes I completely lost my temper and told them to shut up and then one of them peed in his pants.

KAREN: Which one?

VALESKA: The fat one. I feel bad because I love him that little fat kid. He's hilarious. I love him and I made him wet his pants in front of all of his friends. I tried to apologize to them. But it was too sophisticated a gesture. I don't know. I think I'm going to get into trouble for it. I might be fired. Those kids. Ha! They hate me. And I can't blame them.

NETTA: No. That's crazy. They love you. I'm sure of it. It will be OK.

KAREN: At my job no one even remembers my name. They all call me Claire. Or Katherine. // People who I've been there for longer than them.

GINA: Are you serious?

VALESKA: I still can't believe you are still working at that place.

KAREN: What do you mean?

VALESKA: It's beneath you.

KAREN: It's what?

VALESKA: Beneath you.

KAREN: I don't believe in that.

VALESKA: What do you mean you don't believe in it?

KAREN: That anything is beneath me. I don't think there is any such thing. Not from my perspective.

VALESKA: And what is your perspective?

KAREN: … Like a grain of sand? Like a root. A rock. Anything like that. Anything that is low and close to the ground.

VALESKA: You should think better of yourself Karen.

KAREN: You don't understand.

VALESKA: I *understand* that you should leave the soup firm Karen. We all think so. No one else will tell you but I will tell you. You are a brilliant woman and you should be doing something more satisfying with your life.

KAREN: (THE WHOLE IDEA OF IT BREAKING HER HEART) But I don't want to leave the soup firm. Why should I leave the soup firm? And anyway what else would I do? It's beautiful in there. In the morning, it's like the Wild West. And that *is* where I learned to use both of my hands at once. No. I don't want to leave the soup firm. I just want the butcher to remember my name. That's all. Otherwise I'm happy there.

VALESKA: If you say so.

KAREN: I do. I say so.

VALESKA: OK, if you're happy.

KAREN: I am, I'm happy.

VALESKA: OK …

KAREN: … OK.

BEAT. BEAT.

NETTA: And how's Will?

KAREN: I don't know. I haven't heard from him.

NETTA: And Fred?

VALESKA: I haven't heard anything either. Gina?

GINA: No. Nothing.

LITTLE PAUSE.

GINA: I'm going to call Kate. See if they're getting close.

SCENE FOUR

MEANWHILE...
REBECCA IS IN HER BATHROOM SAYING A
LETTER TO HER HUSBAND JACK.

REBECCA: Dear Jack,
Remember when we first met? Remember when we
first met and I would meet you at the cafe? How I
would ride my bike all the way there sometimes, how
sometimes I would ride it so fast. God I was young
then. It wasn't so long ago, but I was so young then,
so much younger now. Or remember how sometimes
I would tip-toe all the way there from the train station,
just for playing a game, and then how I would get
there and drink someone else's coffee? I feel like I'm
drinking someone else's coffee now Jack. I feel like—
Remember how we used to laugh? Fuck you Jack.
What are you doing out there? Where are you?

SCENE FIVE

MEANWHILE...
IN THE CAR WITH KATE AND THE NEW GIRL.
AN AWKWARD SILENCE.

KATE: I'm sorry I'm not feeling so talkative this morning.

PAUSE.

KATE: Honestly I'm not sure why they picked me to pick you up.

PAUSE.

KATE: Don't get me wrong, I'm happy to do it, but I'm in one of the stages of deployment that is— *(LIGHTLY)* well, let's just say it is *not* characterized by feelings of confidence and well-being.

NEW GIRL: That's OK. How long has your husband been away?

KATE: A while now.

PAUSE.
A LITTLE MORE PAUSE.

KATE: So, how did you find out about us anyway?

NEW GIRL: A neighbor told me.

KATE: Oh that's good. It's good to know at least three of your neighbors. You may need their help in emergency situations. And they can offer support on a day to day basis too.

NEW GIRL: What kinds of emergency situations?

KATE: Oh just, you know, if something happens with your kids. Or if you have a breakdown or something like that.

NEW GIRL: A breakdown?

KATE: Your car or. If you just need to talk to someone. It's nothing to worry about. You'll be OK.

ANOTHER LITTLE PAUSE.

NEW GIRL: I don't have any kids.

KATE: Me either.

NEW GIRL: I have a dog.

KATE: Oh that's great! I have a cat. Wow, you have really good instincts. You know your neighbors already and you have a pet? I had to be told all of these things. I didn't come by it naturally at all. What kind of a dog is it?

NEW GIRL: A dachshund? A dachshund I think. I don't know really. We got him at the animal rescue.

KATE: … I think if it was a dachshund you'd know.

NEW GIRL: Why?

KATE: Because they're a very particular—They have those tiny legs I think. Right? Aren't they the little brown dogs that have very long bodies and very short legs?

NEW GIRL: Oh, then it isn't a dachshund. It's gray and, not so long but it's—it is short but it's got wiry gray hair and it looks like it's wearing a mustache.

KATE: That sounds like a schnauzer.

NEW GIRL: Yes that sounds right! A schnauzer.

KATE: What's its name?

NEW GIRL: Skipjack.

KATE: That's cute. Aw that's cute. My cat's name is Eudora.

NEW GIRL: Eudora?

KATE: Yep. Eudora. We're almost there. It's OK. They're really nice girls.

KATE: Hello?

GINA: Kate?

KATE: Gina?

GINA: Yeah we're here are you almost here?

KATE: Almost, I just picked up—

NEW GIRL: Margerie.

KATE: Margerie, sorry, and we're about … half-way there I guess. You guys should probably go ahead and start without us, we're running into some traffic so. We might be a little bit late.

GINA: You're already a little bit late.

KATE: Sorry.

GINA: It's OK.

KATE: Do you guys need anything? Some half and half or?

GINA: No I think we have everything. Does anybody need anything? Kate and the new girl // are about half way here.

KATE: Margerie.

KAREN: If they go by a gas station could you ask them to get
             me some Twizzlers? I don't know why but I'm having a
             craving for Twizzlers right now.

GINA: Could you get Karen some Twizzlers?

KATE: OK. See you in a bit.

GINA: She says we should go ahead and start.

KATE: They want us to bring some Twizzlers.

VALESKA: You're having a craving? At ten in the morning? For
             candy?

KAREN: I guess so.

VALESKA: Are you pregnant?

KAREN: Do I look pregnant?

NETTA: I don't think we should start if there's a new girl
             coming. I think we should wait for them to get here.

MEANWHILE...

REBECCA: You would be proud of me lately. I made it outside
             twice yesterday. And last night, I slept in the bed. The
             sky turned pink after I talked to you last and I thought
             maybe you had sent me that, that pink sky, to try to
             make me smile. Like the time you brought in all that
             sand from the beach, and when you brought me a tree
             to sit under in the living room.

             I only lost the keys twice last week. And only once
             I couldn't find what I was looking for. But I made
             it outside twice yesterday is it Tuesday? I think it's
             Tuesday and so yesterday would be Monday and
             tomorrow will be Wednesday and I'm trying to keep
             track. Of that sort of thing better.

I admitted how I was feeling! And everybody said, they loved me. Which only made it worse. But I didn't tell them this time. So that is an improvement, right?

It's just
simple things
I can't do…

Pull back the curtains. I am trying with all my might to pull back the curtains Jack or at least. That's what I say I am doing. Maybe I only think I am trying so hard because something inside me hurts so bad. But I'm talking. To people about it. And I went outside twice today. I mean. Yesterday. And this morning, I had a glass of juice. Mixed with juice.

MEANWHILE…

GINA: … And she says, Are you in line? And I say, Yes. And she says, Well you better move up there or else someone is going to come along and get in front of us. And so I say to the guy in front of me, Are you in line? And he says, Yes. And so I say to her, I'm standing behind him because he's in front of me, and she gives me this dirty look. Whatever. We wait a while.

And then the guy in front of me, he gets tired of waiting and he leaves. And so then she just—the woman she just gets right in front of me. As if we hadn't just had this whole conversation. As if it were her right to just do that!

And then she goes about to make friends with the woman in front of her! Yeah, they start to talk about how she went to see the Manhattan Transfer once at Madison Square Garden and all of this kind of thing and I thought, What? Is it because I'm white? Is it because you're old? And then she won't look at me again for the whole rest of the hour that we waited. I mean. It made me furious! I was totally—furious, and all I could think was I hope you're happy. I hope you're happy, that was all I could think. I couldn't think of anything to say to her, I couldn't think of what to do!

I didn't know how long we were going to be there and so I didn't want to start anything that might get ugly but oh! I was just miserable! And so I just stared at her. The whole time I just—stared at the back of her head and tried to—punish her and make her—suffer with my—energy. Yeah! That's what I was doing with my energy! I don't want to do that with my energy! (But I think it worked a little, I think she did feel kind of ashamed.) But ulgh! It was ridiculous! And I know everybody else in the line, who hadn't seen what had happened but who could see the way I was staring at this woman, oh my god they must have thought I was a monster! But I am not a monster but I mean come on! What is that all about? What did she think? Because she had a cane? I would've let her in front of me anyway. If she'd just asked I would have let her in front of me, but under the circumstances I didn't see how being one person further along was going to help her out that much! So I felt stupid offering! But anyway! And then she gets in front of me anyway! But anyway, under normal circumstances I am actually the kind of person who does that, who lets the elderly get in front of me in line, at the grocery store or wherever, but these were not normal circumstances // it didn't seem to me.

VALESKA: This is what you would rather talk about than talking about the weather?

GINA: I didn't say I didn't want to talk about the weather.

KAREN: But wait a minute. I don't get this. What is this a story about anyway?

GINA: Isn't it obvious?

KAREN: Isn't it obvious that it isn't?

NETTA: No it's about violence. Right? Between the races. The generation gap. Cruelty. And being ineffectual. It's about city life. Disrespect and so forth. The entitlements of the aged. Isn't it? Isn't that what it's about?

GINA: I don't know what it's about I'm just talking. Aren't we just waiting for everyone else to get here, what am I? Supposed to be the entertainment?

KAREN: Yeah where the hell is everybody?

NETTA: Could you guys please stop cussing?!

GINA: *(TO KAREN)* She's trying to quit.

KAREN: Call Rebecca.

GINA CALLS REBECCA. HER ANSWERING MACHINE PICKS UP: "HI, THIS IS REBECCA AND HALF THE TIME JACK. IF THIS CALL IS GOING TO MAKE MY DAY BETTER PLEASE LEAVE A MESSAGE. IF NOT, PLEASE CALL SOMEBODY ELSE." BEEP.

GINA: Rebecca? You there? It's me Gina, Rebecca. Pick up the phone.

GINA PACES.

NETTA: You guys want a donut?

KAREN: Yeah I'll have a donut.

VALESKA: No thank you.

GINA: Are you there? Rebecca? Pick up the phone.

NETTA GETS THE DONUTS. SHE EATS ONE WHILE SHE TALKS.

NETTA: But that story. It reminds me. This story isn't about city life or anything like that but. Have I ever told you guys about my sister?

VALESKA: I didn't know you had a sister.

GINA: She's not picking up.

NETTA: Oh yeah. Disaster. Unbelievable disaster. Desperate, desperate person and full of lies. And deceit you know. Would do anything to get attention. Just anything. She would make these jokes all the time. And sing. She had this incredible singing voice and she was always—showing it off. And she would dance and she had these great moves and she would tell these funny stories, she had this incredible memory and she would tell these really long, detailed stories from her memory about our childhood and they were always a real crack-up the way she remembered everything. And also she was like. She was a people person. She just loved people. Anybody. All of them! Everyone. It didn't matter what they were like, it didn't matter if they were poor or creepy or whatever she could always find something in them to like. And she played sports! She was on one of these community leagues where they would meet in the park on the same day at the same time over a period of years, yeah she could really—keep things going like that—and oh! Oh my god she was a volunteer! Yes! She was a really good cook, and she could sew, and she vol-un-teered—at the post office, once a week she would go down there to the post office and she would deliver the mail—for free! Because the post office is going out of business you know, // and so she would do that

VALESKA: I didn't know that.

NETTA: Oh yeah // and so she would do that

KAREN: I didn't know that either.

NETTA: And also—also she taught grade school! Yes. Special needs kids of course. Elghck. She was just—horrible. Really. An embarrassment to the whole family. A real shame.

LITTLE PAUSE.

VALESKA: Is she dead?

NETTA: What?

VALESKA: Is she dead? Because you keep talking about her in the past tense.

NETTA: ... I do?

VALESKA: Yes.

NETTA: ... No. No she's not dead. God. That's weird.

KAREN: Speaking of the past tense, did I tell you guys? I'm learning Japanese.

GINA: You are?

KAREN: Yeah.

GINA: Wow that's great.

KAREN: Yeah I really like it.

VALESKA: When did you start doing that?

KAREN: About a week ago.

NETTA: Say something! Say something in Japanese.

VALESKA: Yes say something.

KAREN: No I don't really know anything yet.

VALESKA: Oh come on just one word.

GINA: Konichiwa!

KAREN: ... Konichiwa.

NETTA: What does it mean?

GINA: It means hello!

KAREN: *(TO GINA)* I know. *(TO EVERYONE)* It means hello.

NETTA: Well I think that's great. Which one is that? Rule number one? Set some goals for yourself as a whole person

NETTA &
KAREN: and then pursue your self-development program

NETTA,
KAREN &
VALESKA: whether or not your husband is at home.

GINA: *(UNDER, WHILE THEY'RE ALL SAYING THE RULE)* blahblahblah blah blah blahblah

WHEN THEY'RE DONE:

GINA: Blaaaaaaccchchhhh! I hate that fuckin rule.

NETTA: Really Gina, please! Stop doing that! *(CUSSING)*

GINA: Sorry.

LITTLE BEAT.

VALESKA: I think I will have one of those donuts now. If there are any left.

NETTA: Oh yeah there's plenty.

MEANWHILE...
KATE HAS PULLED THE CAR OVER AND IS SORT
OF HOLDING THE NEW GIRL HOSTAGE.

KATE: I'm sorry. I didn't mean for this to happen. I just wanted to take you to the meeting and introduce you to the girls. They're great. They're great people and all that but honestly, if I'm to be perfectly honest with you, which is a part of our pact, then I would have to tell you honestly that I just don't think I can go there today.

It's a horrible life Margerie. I just want you to know that upfront. Your husband is probably a wonderful man but. Being a submariner's wife—

Look. I'm not a bad person. I'm not a bad person but—

KATE TELLS THE FOLLOWING STORY TO THE NEW GIRL. REBECCA TELLS BASICALLY THE SAME STORY TO JACK. THEY SPEAK THE ITALICIZED LINES TOGETHER, IN IMPERFECT UNISON. REBECCA IS FOREGROUNDED IN THIS DUET.

REBECCA: The walls are falling away from the floors, Jack. // The walls are falling away from the floors and

KATE: The walls are falling away from the floors in my apartment, Margerie. And sometimes I dream what that will be like, when they actually do fall.

REBECCA: I don't know when is the right time to have someone come over and check about that. *Is it tomorrow? The next day?* // When you get home?

KATE: When he gets home?

REBECCA: I'm afraid I'm going to wait until *just that moment too long—I'm afraid I'm going to call like, right at the moment I've got cancer is the moment I'll actually quit smoking. I'm afraid I'm going to call about the walls right at that moment before.* // The guy will come over in his tool belt, and we'll stand in the living room and he'll say, What seems to be the problem? And I'll say, Well…

KATE: So I called this guy finally. And he came over. He was wearing a tool belt and he said, What seems to be the trouble? And I said, Well *it's … the walls, they're coming away from the floors you can see. If you look, here, and here… There's all this space that clearly wasn't here when the house was built and I think, if I'm not mistaken or crazy, either of which is possible,* and

I laugh, and he laughs and I say, *I think that the space there is getting bigger. Expanding. Which is a matter of some concern because—I could lose something down there or—if the walls collapse, then what will become of the neighbors? //* He checks it out and he says, Well it is an old house after all, I don't think it's anything to worry about. And then

REBECCA: And he'll check it out and he'll say, Well it is an old house after all I don't think it's anything to worry about. And then, just then, right at that moment, is when there they'll go. The walls will just—drop away from the house, and the sky will come—flooding in. And there we'll be. Me, and the guy in the tool belt. Standing in the living room on the third floor of the air *with the leaves blowing in around us. And a bird will come and land there on the rug* and I'll say, It's beautiful. I wish my husband were here to see it.

KATE: And then I said, Well if you don't think it's any problem, do you want a glass of milk? And he says yes and so I get it for him. He drinks it and puts the glass down, and then he kisses me. The guy in the tool belt. He kisses me. Full on the mouth. It comes as a surprise. But I let him. I had to let him. You don't understand.

REBECCA: This morning, Jack, I was lachrymose.

KATE: Maybe someday you'll understand.

REBECCA: I smeared a tear into the wood floor with the bottom of my slipper.

KATE: Or maybe you'll maybe never have to understand.

NEW GIRL: I'm sorry but. I'm not sure I know what you're telling me.

REBECCA: I go down to the canal by myself sometimes.

KATE: I'm having an affair Margerie.

REBECCA: I go down to the canal and I watch the boats.

KATE: I'm sleeping with the guy in the tool belt.

REBECCA: The sail boats.

KATE: The guy who drank our milk.

REBECCA: The kayaks.

KATE: I'm having an affair with him is what I'm trying to tell you.

REBECCA: The one-man sculls.

LITTLE PAUSE.

NEW GIRL: Well. I'd still like to go to the meeting. // If you don't mind. If you wouldn't mind dropping me off there at least. I'd still like to go.

REBECCA: They gleam in the morning. They sparkle. They shine.

KATE: Yes! Absolutely! You should go! It's no problem. It's no problem at all. Wow. I feel so much better now... Maybe I'll even go with you.

MEANWHILE...

NETTA: But anyway god she was awful. And I just thought: What is the matter with this girl? Why can't she be happy with her own mind? In her own skin? She hates it. Her teeth. She hates our parents. And all of our uncles. And all of our dead friends. Our church. Why can't she just be happy drinking this glass of water, looking out this window at this goddamn fucking goddamn fucking fuck fuck magnolia tree which is in bloom, and some people might say was put there just for goddamn fucking fuck fuck her pleasure? Why not? Why she hates her face and all that and whatnot, why she's always getting this sand kicked in her eyes or so she thinks? So she never could do the splits so so so

31

what? So she never could dress right or say the right thing or ask the right question or give the right answer who cares?! So she always had these shitty friends who didn't care about her and who never really knew her and who were jealous and competitive and unkind and stingy and forgetful and drug addicts and drunks and criminals and who couldn't drive, not a stinking last one of 'em. And so they were ugly! Ugliest goddamn group of people you ever saw so what so there wasn't one single person beautiful or even handsome or even attractive, now here's an attractive boy or she's an attractive girl so there wasn't even one single person could be described like that in a hundred mile radius of where we grew up who cares!? All pig farmers and auto mechanics, every last one of 'em pig farmers and auto mechanics and their slutty, dirty sisters—and daughters—and cousins—and mothers—so what!?

KAREN: I just don't see how God could make a creature that hated itself. I just don't see the beauty in that.

VALESKA: Well your first problem with that the trouble is in believing in God.

GINA: That one guy, I hate that one guy who is always running around trying to cheer everybody up all the time. Do you guys know about this? What is his name. He's kind of famous right now but I think he's like a total— fascist. Or whatever that—other word is.

KATE AND THE NEW GIRL ENTER.

KATE: We made it!

NEW GIRL: Barely.

KATE: Oh, shit. We forgot the Twizzlers.

SHLOMY APPEARS. HE TALKS TO THE AUDIENCE
ABOUT HIS BROTHER, WHO WANTED TO FLY.

SHLOMY: It was
            he was like
            he loved
            anything that was in the air
            or of the air
            and he loved anything
            that was in the water
            or of the water
            but he didn't care so much
            for anything in between.
            He had

            Once I remember he had
            gone through this week where
            he was continually observing all of these horrors that
            were being inflicted on pigeons. Inflicted by cars, or
            by falling objects, or in some cases, even by other
            pigeons.

            Every day he would call me on the phone and tell me
            another one of these stories. Stories about pigeons
            smashed flat on the sidewalk, stories about pigeons
            hobbling around in the park, dragging their legs
            and wings behind them. Once! He saw a pigeon ...
            assassination. He cried into my answering machine
            for ten minutes telling me that story. About how one
            pigeon pushed another's egg from a nest and how he
            watched the egg fall and break open on the ground
            and how the mother pigeon went crazy and was
            running all around in circles like she was going crazy.
            And then once, a decapitated pigeon fell out of the sky
            and landed right at his feet. He said: This is a horrible
            place. Where these kinds of things can happen.

            Anyway.

            He had

            Apparently he had been building himself a one-man
            submersible. He had rented a shed from a neighbor
            and he spent all his time in there working on it. We
            didn't know anything about it but that wasn't unusual
            but yeah.

He built this little—submarine for himself, that he could pedal underwater and around the river like a bike. A little vessel, with a window in it so he could look out into the sea, into the under-water, and be a part of it all. It had these little … fins on the sides, sticking out from the sides like—penguin arms, like—wings.

But uhm…

It didn't fly.
It sank.
And he went down with it.

MEANWHILE…

REBECCA: I made it outside twice yesterday. And this morning, I had a glass of juice mixed with juice. That's progress, isn't it? Isn't that progress?

HORACE HUNLEY ENTERS.

HORACE: I think so.

REBECCA: Horace Hunley! You came.

HORACE: I brought a movie.

REBECCA: Oh that's a good idea. I can bring the TV in here too. And the VCR.

HORACE: Yeah it's the one about that small town guy who thinks he's a flop and wishes he'd never been born.

REBECCA: I don't think I've seen it. *(WRY)* Though it sounds familiar.

HORACE: Really? Oh you're in for a real treat. In the end // he's surprised to find—

REBECCA: No don't tell me the end!

HORACE: No it won't spoil it—He's surprised to find that he does actually fit into the scheme of things, and that he contributed much to the happiness of several people. I think you'll be able to associate yourself with him. And perhaps you'll feel a little bit better for having known him.

REBECCA: *(SKEPTICAL)* ... Maybe.

> SHE OPENS THE MEDICINE CABINET. OR GOES
> TO THE MEDICINE CABINET. OR THINKS ABOUT
> EVERYTHING THAT'S IN THE MEDICINE CABINET.

REBECCA: Do you want a band-aid?

HORACE: Sure, I'll have a band-aid.

REBECCA: I had a dream that everything was so fertile Horace. That everything I planted last year was growing and in bloom this year. But it was almost like it was too green. Too alive. Then I was blindfolded. I almost danced. But I was on the edge of something, a table that was also the edge of the earth. It was exhilarating. Profound. Too much. I was paralyzed. Out of breath. Frightened. A flock of birds flew by and knocked me over. On purpose. They didn't want to share that part of the sky with me. I thought: I can't touch anything. Because it will break.

HORACE: I think we should just use the simple minimum of words we can possibly use. We should start now, and we should just use the absolute
simple
minimum.

REBECCA: Help.

HORACE: Trying.

REBECCA: Hurts.

HORACE: Yes. Yes Linda it does hurt. That's true.

REBECCA: I don't think that was the absolute simple minimum Horace. And also, my name's not Linda.

AN AWKWARD PAUSE BETWEEN THEM.

MEANWHILE...
IN THE CONFERENCE ROOM, THE LADIES ARE
DESCRIBING THE VARIOUS STAGES OF DEPLOYMENT
TO THE NEW GIRL. TELLING HER WHAT SHE CAN
EXPECT TO FEEL AND EXPERIENCE AND GIVING HER
ADVICE ABOUT HOW TO COPE AND BEHAVE.

VALESKA: And then there is the stage wherein the petals fall off the flowers. This stage is characterized by feelings of confusion, ambivalence, anger, pulling away. And then there is the stage wherein the stage is covered with grass, thick, bright green grass, and the actress is very beautiful, and very talented, and the whole audience wants to make out with her, and put their hands up her skirt.

NEW GIRL: I've also heard that it's OK to go to parties where singles will be present. That I should wear my wedding ring to prevent confusion and criticism, but that it's still OK to attend.

VALESKA: Well yes you are a mature adult and you are capable of conversations and relationships with both men and women.

KAREN: But you probably shouldn't go to singles' bars. If you do, you're just asking for trouble.

VALESKA: I don't follow that rule. I go to singles' bars if I want to. I am not afraid of them.

KATE AND REBECCA SAY THE FOLLOWING TEXT TOGETHER.
KATE IS TALKING TO MARGERIE. REBECCA IS TALKING
TO HORACE. THEY ARE BASICALLY EXPLAINING HOW
THEY TRY TO GET THROUGH THE DAY SOMETIMES.

KATE & REBECCA:	Every day I wake up and I make a plan. This morning the magnolia tree is blooming, starting to bloom—I didn't have anything to do with that. I tell myself: today it's going to be a good day. I'm going to take care of some things. I'm going to get some things done I'm going to feel good about myself. I'm going to do some things that will make me feel good about myself and I'm going to do some things that I need to do, some things I ought to have done already, some of my responsibilities, I'm going to take care of some of those—yeah. One everyday thing, one special thing for me, and one big responsibility thing. Like dishes and flowers and taxes. And then I think this feeling of capacity will start to grow in me. I'll sit still and be quiet for ten minutes and think about other people. Other people who have it worse than I do. For ten minutes I will sit down and not talk and not think about myself. I'll listen to the birds and try to connect with the nature. Look up into the sky and remember what a big world it is and what a small small part of it I really am.
GINA:	Oh yeah. That's what I'll do. That's a great idea. I'll consider my own irrelevance. That's a good plan. Whose idea was that anyway? Your mother's? What sadistic tradition did that little gem of wisdom grow out of? Yuk!
KATE:	I know it seems optimistic, Gina, but if you tried it, maybe you'd feel a little better.
GINA:	I feel fine. Kate. I feel just fine.
KAREN:	Also, you can't just have sex with yourself whenever you want to. You've got to work up to it. You've got to—do something to make yourself interesting to yourself. Otherwise it's just a—what? It's like a free-for-all.
NEW GIRL:	That makes sense.

NETTA: What was that thing you were talking about before? On the phone with your job. // What is this case you're following?

GINA: A bridge collapse.

NETTA: What were the effects? // What became of the community? *(TRAILING OFF)* How long did it take to rebuild? Did anyone die? Are they still dead?

VALESKA: And you should remember also to know other kinds of people. Like poets.

KAREN: And basketball players.

KATE: And high school students.

VALESKA: Otherwise you can think that it is a very small world out there and that it is only water, and waiting, and wondering.

GINA: *(JOINING THE GROUP, RESPONDING TO VALESKA)* It isn't?

VALESKA: We've just named at least three other things that exist.

GINA: Poets and basketball players and foreign exchange students?

VALESKA: High school. She said, high school. They don't have to be foreign exchange.

KAREN: *(TO THE NEW GIRL)* I have this watercolor? In my kitchen? It's of a sunset and it has a rowboat in it. I dream sometimes. Daydream. That I am rowboating off into that watercolored sunset. And do you know what? It's right now. I'm dreaming it right now.

NETTA: *(ALSO TO THE NEW GIRL)* Getting my mind to work. Getting my mind to work properly. I'd say that's probably my number one frustration.

MEANWHILE...

HORACE: ... And this blind dog doesn't even know what it's barking at! And then, this woman, this exquisite, perfectly shaped like a sundae black woman says to me You want to buy a beautiful poem for a dollar? And I say, No, and I give her a dollar, and the poem is called: "I Wish I Could Be of More Help." And do you want to know what her name is? The poet?

REBECCA: Astrid—Amanda—Pinkerton.

HORACE: N-no. Her name is Robin Williams. This improbable black woman living on the street selling poems for a dollar is named Robin Williams. Can you believe that?

REBECCA: ... What kind of paper was it on?

HORACE: What?

REBECCA: The poem. What kind of paper was it on?

HORACE: Paper. It was on—plain white. Eight and a half by eleven.

REBECCA: ... I wonder where she got it.

HORACE: You're curious. You're a curious person Rebecca.

REBECCA: It's true.

HORACE: I like that.

REBECCA SMILES.
MEANWHILE...
THE NEW GIRL HAS BEEN TELLING THE LADIES
THAT SHE IS LEARNING TO BE A HYPNOTIST.

KAREN: Do you think you could do it to us?

NEW GIRL: I don't know I guess I could—give it a try. All right you'll
                have to—Everyone just relax. And think of something
                that will help you relax.

PAUSE WHILE THE NEW GIRL WAITS FOR THEM TO RELAX.

VALESKA: *(QUIET)* Excuse me. I have to go to the bathroom.

VALESKA LEAVES.

NEW GIRL: *(GENTLE)* You're crazy.
                You have a crazy life.
                I mean—
                Did I say you were crazy?
                I didn't mean to say that.

                If I say something wrong just—incorporate it into
                the procedure. My mistakes—will only make you go
                deeper into the state of relaxation which allows you to
                access your subconscious mind, making it easier for
                you to take the suggestions I am making—WHICH
                ARE IN NO WAY AGAINST YOUR PRINCIPLES OR
                BELIEFS—but are perfectly acceptable to you. And
                even, desirable.

                You have a crazy life. And you live in a crazy city. But
                this will not make *you* crazy. *You* are not crazy. (In
                spite of what I said before.)

                There is too much money here. And you will never
                have any of it. No one will understand you, and you
                will never have any money, and you won't care. Any
                more. You can be at parties, where other people are
                there understanding each other and being understood
                and having lots of money, but that is OK—with *you.*
                You won't need to do that—just because other people
                need to do that.

                You will never have a normal life. And that is OK with
                you too. That is great with you. You will love your
                abnormal life the way an abnormal tiger mother loves

its abnormal tiger baby. You can be at parties, with other tigers who are normal tigers and you won't even bat an eye, it won't matter to you one bit because *you*—are abnormal. And that is the way it was meant to be, and that is the way it is, and that is the way it will always be.

GINA: *(ENJOYING IT)* It feels like someone's putting pins in me.

MEANWHILE...

REBECCA: And then this very old woman, very old, and
Hi, what are you doing?
I'm just sitting here.
You're so old.
So what?
So old.
So what.
You must know something.
I don't know anything.
But you must know something.
I don't.
But you're so old.
Get away from me you crazy bitch.
Etcetera.

HORACE: Well yes Linda. The world is hostile. Resplendent. And small. Are you good at anything?

REBECCA: Are you?

HORACE: Well uhm. I was. I used to be. I uh ...

REBECCA: Yeah. Me too.

PAUSE.

REBECCA: There are all those *rooms*. You know? Out there. Past this one? And I just—think—What is happening in them? When I'm not in them?

HORACE: It's impossible to know.

REBECCA: And so then I just. Don't know where to *be*. In relation
            to everything. There is so much … *information* in
            everything. And this is only just in the one house I'm
            talking about! And so then I think well outside the
            house it is only more of the same and then I—

HORACE: Unh-hunh unh-hunh unh-hunh unh-hunh—

REBECCA: Yeah. Right and so—

HORACE: Unh-hunh—

REBECCA: Right and so—

HORACE: Yeah.

> *BACK IN THE CONFERENCE ROOM, THE LADIES ARE
> RESTING IN THEIR POST-HYPNOTIC STATES.*

> *THE WHOLE STAGE IS VERY STILL.*

> *SUDDENLY, KAREN HAS AN EMOTIONAL EMERGENCY,
> AN INSUPPRESSIBLE NEED TO SHARE.*

KAREN: *(STANDING UP)* My husband won't touch me.

GINA: Shh. Stop, wait.

> *PAUSE. THEY WAIT.*

GINA: This moment. This moment right here? Is perfect.

> *NOT FOR KAREN. SHE LEAVES.*

> *MEANWHILE…*

HORACE: I didn't know how to drive and so I was—giving myself
            driving lessons. I borrowed a car from my mother's
            boyfriend, my mother's boyfriend who says I don't
            know how anyone can live in this city for one minute

and not fall in love with a waitress! And I say, One minute? and he says, OK ten! And he loans me his car, because he's that kind of a guy, who goes to costume parties dressed up as a moth and falls in love with waitresses and leaves my mother for them. He loans me his car because I want to learn how to drive and he says, OK Horace, here are the keys, they go in there. Have a good time! And so I'm driving it around. And I'm not doing a very good job. And I'm ashamed, I have to admit, because I'm old, you know, to be learning something like this.

Other people, they come from places where they can't believe someone my age doesn't know how to drive. And I say to them, Well I can't believe you don't know any black people. But they don't know what I mean by this, they don't get it. But anyway I'm trying at least which is more than I can say for them. And so I'm on the corner of that—street where the Russian baths are? The real ones, not the ones where there aren't actually any Russian people. But I'm there on the corner there and there's a train overhead and—

REBECCA: I love a train.

HORACE: Yeah. And it distracts me and—

REBECCA: Any train.

HORACE: Yeah and the next thing I know—

REBECCA: Going anywhere.

HORACE: R-right. And so the next thing I know, I've crashed Max's car into a girl.

REBECCA: Oh.

HORACE: A girl in a headscarf riding a bicycle with a basket with a parakeet in a cage in it. And she's got a purse. Or she had a purse. And the purse had a lipstick in it I know, because now the purse is out on the street in front of the car next to the birdcage, and the bike and the girl and the lipstick is there too. And you can see from the way everything landed that the lipstick came out of the purse and the girl came off of the bike and the birdcage came out of the basket—but thank god the bird is still in the cage—and the girl is not dead, and her headscarf is there, right there, next to her hair.

I run over and I want to see if everyone's all right. And I'm yelling. For some reason I'm yelling I'm sorry! I don't know how to drive! This is my mother's boyfriend's car! I'm sorry! I mean ex-boyfriend. He fell in love with a waitress. Are you OK?

People start to come around and ask what's going on and I say I grew up here, I'm sorry, I don't know how to drive. But I was trying to learn and now I've, I'm sorry, and so on, and Do you think she's OK?

I ran over to her.

REBECCA: Naturally.

HORACE: I'm not a monster.

REBECCA: Of course not.

HORACE: I ran over her. And then I ran over to her.

When she comes to, she's bleeding a little, from here (HE TOUCHES THE PLACE ON REBECCA'S FACE WHERE THE WOMAN WAS BLEEDING)—but not too bad. And I put my hand there. And she smiles a little. Like she was waking up from something—

REBECCA: Which she was.

HORACE: But she smiled like she was waking up from something else. And now, when she smiles, she wakes up in my apartment. She lives with me now and when she wakes up, she smiles like she's just been hit by a car. And I make her toast in the mornings, and tell her every day that it's all right, that she's all right, that it's going to be all right. Even though I'm not sure it's true.

REBECCA: That isn't your story, Horace.

Tell me the story of your life in three words. And an object.

HORACE: Water. Water. Water. And a glass of water. Tell me yours.

REBECCA: ... I wouldn't know where to begin.

HORACE: How about at the beginning?

REBECCA: ... I don't know where it is.

KAREN COMES BACK TO THE CONFERENCE ROOM,
HER NEED TO SHARE STILL INTACT.

KAREN: My husband won't touch me because I told him not to. Well, I didn't tell him in so many words. In fact, I didn't tell him in any words at all. But every time he would touch me, I would sort of—wince. Or kind of—flinch? I'm ticklish. So he's stopped touching me. And I can't blame him. After he stopped touching me, I stopped touching me too. And now, I sort of have this body but. I'm not really using it.

On Thursdays, they come by here and take up stuff you don't want anymore that someone else might be able to use. Do you guys think they'd take my body, if I left it out there, in a bag, with the shoes and the coffee maker?

NO ONE SAYS ANYTHING. MAYBE THEY ALL KNOW
THIS FEELING. IT WILL PASS.

KAREN LEAVES AGAIN.

NETTA: So. Margerie. Why don't you tell us where you met *your* husband.

MARGERIE: Oh.
He used to come into the place where I worked.
Every day.
Sometimes twice.
It was his arms. When I saw his arms, that's what did it. I started working there in the winter. And the winters there are very long. There are very long winters there and so for many months he would come in and he would be wearing long sleeves. Of course. Long sleeved sweaters or long sleeved shirts with long sleeved … jackets over them and, or, then a winter coat on top of that. Also I noticed—I guess the first thing I noticed was that—well, no, I was going to say the first thing I noticed was that his voice was astonishingly deep. But that's not actually true. It's not really "astonishing" but. It is really deep. He has a very, very deep voice. Maybe the deepest voice I've ever heard. And he would never smile at me for some reason. He says because he's shy. He was shy. I made him feel shy. And sometimes he would even try to come in and go out without having to interact with me. But I wouldn't let that happen. Unh-unh. No way.

AT SOME POINT DURING MARGERIE'S STORY, WE SEE HORACE AND REBECCA WATCHING "IT'S A WONDERFUL LIFE" ON THE TV-VCR WHICH SHE'S BROUGHT INTO THE BATHROOM. THEY'RE ENJOYING IT.

MEANWHILE,
KAREN IS OFF ALONE SOMEWHERE, STANDING VERY STILL, LOOKING OUT AND UP INTO A BRIGHT LIGHT. WE HEAR THE VOICE OF THE JAPANESE, BUT WE DON'T SEE HIM.

THE
JAPANESE: And, so, why do you want to learn Japanese, Karen?

KAREN: Because I. Because of my mind. Because I want to learn new ways of using my mind. Because I'm tired of all the old familiar ways that my mind wants to use itself. Because I want to make new pathways. Forge new paths. Like a barbarian almost, chopping away at the wilderness. I want to chop away at the wilderness of my mind. Like someone with a machete. Hacking through bramble. Hacking through the bramble of my mind. I want to learn new ways to think. And I can't think—I think that Japanese will help me with this because. The Japanese, they—

THE
JAPANESE: "The Japanese"?

KAREN: They think so differently from me. The thinking seems so ... elegant. But unruly. Dignified, yet—

THE
JAPANESE: Uhn-hunh.

KAREN: And the language is the system of thinking, right? Or the voice of the thinking is the language, right? Or the thinking is the. The language is the.

THE
JAPANESE: *(CUTTING HER OFF, HELPING HER OUT)* OK Karen. Before you go hacking away at your mind with a machete, I suggest you read this little book.

KAREN: OK. What is it called?

THE
JAPANESE: It's called "The Tokyo Yellow Pages."

KAREN: OK. I will read it tonight.

> *THE TOKYO YELLOW PAGES FALLS FROM THE SKY*
> *AND LANDS AT KAREN'S FEET. IT'S HUGE.*

KAREN: Or I will look at it. At least. Or I will sit with it in my lap. At least. For hours. For at least an hour.

THE
JAPANESE: Excellent. I'll see you on Tuesday at one.

MEANWHILE...

REBECCA: Have you ever noticed how, when they're doing a news story, say, on the radio or on television, and they have to report about an accident, or an incident, involving the submarine, have you ever noticed how the reporters kind of—rush through it? How they seem kind of—embarrassed—to have to be reporting about something like that? Like they're doing a *book report* suddenly on the *cotton gin*. Like it's an assignment they give to someone who is trying to climb his way up the ladder. A rookie. Like it's a rookie assignment! Have you ever noticed this? Or like—like it's a kind of punishment for if they've done something wrong like, if maybe on their last story they made up some facts or—mispronounced someone's name and as a kind of punishment then they have to do the *submarine* story now? You can hear it in their voice. There is this— *tone*. They are trying to hide it but they can never hide it. They feel—that the submarine—is irrelevant. Like Jesus. Without the miracles. Or like the oboe! Or the French horn! Or like grammar or like handwriting. It drives me nuts, Horace. It makes me crazy!

HORACE: You want to know what I think is irrelevant? What drives me crazy?

REBECCA: What?

HORACE:

HE CAN'T THINK OF ANYTHING.

HORACE: Rebecca.

REBECCA: Yes, Horace?

HORACE: When's your birthday?

REBECCA: I don't know. June tenth?

SHE KNOWS JUNE TENTH IS HER BIRTHDAY. SHE JUST WASN'T EXPECTING THE QUESTION.

HORACE: Right, June tenth, so that would make you a—

REBECCA: Gemini, Horace! But who cares? And anyway. Enough about me.

HORACE: (AGREEING) Seriously.

REBECCA: So what about you? What happened with you out there? I mean what were you thinking Horace? What on earth were you thinking sending that wreck of a boat back out into the water time and time again? And time and time again and again?

HORACE: I was thinking…
            I hope it works.
            I hope it works this time.

                        MEANWHILE…

            *BACK IN THE CONFERENCE ROOM, IT SEEMS THAT
            MARGERIE'S STORY HAS BEEN GOING ON AND ON.*

MARGERIE: And it would always surprise me and also—It seemed … incongruous. To his face. To his whole … To the way he looked. He has a kind of a boyish face to tell you the truth. Not feminine but. Young in a way. And he is very clean. You know? He is clean shaven, and he wears clean and simple clothes with clean lines. And he wears architect glasses! He is … meticulous. Not fragile. But fine. Everything about him is fine. Like fine furniture or fine glass. And so but then this voice would come out of him. And I don't know it seemed— unlikely. Did I say that already? // And it seemed like it could shatter the fine bone structure of his face

KATE: You said incongruous.

MARGERIE: by coming up from behind like that, out of his… Anyway these things I noticed. Whatever. People have all kinds of things like this. At that job I had then I would see all kinds of people with things like this. Shocking, outrageous, completely unfathomable… I mean it was just an endless, heartbreaking, priceless parade of—

VALESKA: You mean like they were crazy?

MARGERIE: No I mean—what they look like. Just. All the ways of
             them.

GINA: But so anyway you were telling us about his arms.

MARGERIE: Yeah, uhm. I don't think I can talk anymore about it
             right now. Can someone tell me where the bathroom
             is? Show me to the bathroom?

NETTA: Oh yeah it's just down the hall to the left.

             You go out the door and make a left at the end of
             the first hall, then go about two thirds of the way
             down— you'll be in the Civil War room which is a big
             rectangular space and if you go along the back wall
             about two thirds of the way down there's a hallway
             on your right and the bathroom is in that hallway on
             your left-hand side. It's the third door. Past the utility
             closet.

                           MARGERIE EXITS.

                           LITTLE PAUSE.

VALESKA: She has an awful lot of confidence.

                           MEANWHILE…
                 *MARGERIE IS IN THE BATHROOM BEATING
                    THE CRAP OUT OF HERSELF.*

VALESKA: I wish you guys could see the underwear I'm wearing
             right now. They are totally obscene.

                           MEANWHILE…

HORACE: You think you got it bad. I think I got it bad.

REBECCA: We do. We do got it bad. You do and so do I.

HORACE: So what should we do?

50

REBECCA: I could just lie here Horace. I could just lie here. All night.

HORACE: It isn't night, Linda.

REBECCA: And my name's not Linda, Horace.

BACK IN THE CONFERENCE ROOM, THE LADIES ARE KIND OF WRAPPING UP THE MEETING.

NETTA: So basically you should just remember that simple things, simple things help a lot. Don't be afraid to have people over to your house and to cook meals for yourself that you enjoy that your husband hates. And do physical labor. // Physical labor is good.

GINA: Physical labor? Like digging a ditch?

KATE: Yeah! Dig a ditch Margerie!

NETTA: No, not like digging a ditch.

KATE: Build a moat! Build a moat! All the way around your house!

NETTA: Like gardening. Or home repair projects. Not digging a ditch. Jesus.

KATE: All the way around your heart for that matter!

VALESKA: *(TO MARGERIE)* Don't listen to her. She's upset. You can listen to her when she's not so upset.

KATE: I'm not upset.

VALESKA: Why are you so upset today Kate?

KATE: I'm not upset! I was just joking.

*MEANWHILE...
SOME MYSTERIOUS TENSION IS RISING
BETWEEN REBECCA AND HORACE.*

REBECCA: Look! I had a friend once Horace. Had a brain tumor. I spent the whole night in the hospital with him. I wrote to him where he used to live on the seashore outside the city and said, Tell me everything Andy. Tell me anything you want to. Ever. I'm listening.

HORACE: Well I don't see how does that help us now!

REBECCA: You can't talk to me like that!

HORACE: OK but I haven't ever really experienced this, have I? So I don't have any business now trying to have a conversation about it, do I?

REBECCA: What, you're not trapped here! How did you even get in here anyway?

HORACE: Oh like you don't know. Like you don't know about that little window in the back by the hallway next to the closet behind the door. Like you don't know that's always unlocked and you send me a letter like that one you sent, and you think I'm not gonna come in? Think I'm not gonna sneak in in the night and just make sure everything's OK?

REBECCA: You just said it wasn't night!

HORACE: Oh you can pretend to send it from Roger, make your little jokes, make your little fictions, Linda, but I know what's real and what isn't! I know that your life is falling apart! And you know it too! The paint is chipping over here Linda. The wallpaper's peeling the dust is collecting the stairs are collapsing and the furniture is all out of order! And you can say that there is no such thing, but there is—no such thing! As order! It's finite, predictable, dependable, you can count on it, point to it, call it by name, it's demonstrable, specific, quantifiable, not subjective, which seems to be so much in the fashion these days, but *order*—is a *thing*, Linda. And when you see it, you will know it, and you will let out a little gasp, a tiny little gasp of air and you will say, Oh! I see! And: I understand! And then we will not have to be having this stupid conversation anymore. Anymore! We will not have to! And I long for that time. Personally Linda, I long for it!

REBECCA: Well so do I!

HORACE: Well so do I!

REBECCA: Well so do I!

HORACE: Well so do I!

REBECCA: Well so do I!

HORACE: Hm!

REBECCA: Hm!

HORACE: Hm!

REBECCA: Hm!

HORACE: Ha!

REBECCA: Ha!

HORACE: Hunh!

REBECCA: Please stop poking me Horace! Please stop poking me from the afterlife with that sharp stick!

BACK IN THE CONFERENCE ROOM.

WE SEE TIM LEAVING THE CONFERENCE ROOM WITH THE POTTED PLANT. THE VERY LARGE POTTED PLANT WHICH HAS BEEN THERE ALL ALONG.

WHEN HE'S GONE:

VALESKA: I think there is something wrong with that guy.

NETTA: Tim? You think there's something wrong with Tim?

VALESKA: I don't know what his name is but I think there's something wrong with him.

NETTA: His name is Tim.

KAREN: I think he has some kind of mental illness. Isn't he mentally ill?

NETTA: I don't know. I don't think so.

VALESKA: I think he's dangerous.

KAREN: Didn't he used to work at the … Aqua Park?

NETTA: Did he?

KAREN: I think so. I think my friend Sharon's daughter worked with him there one summer. I think she thought he was strange.

VALESKA: Yes he is strange. I see him all the time looking at women—

GINA: That's strange?

VALESKA: And he has an erection.

GINA: Oh.

VALESKA: It's creepy.

NETTA: When do you see him all the time looking at women? When do you see him with an erection?

VALESKA: When I'm in the hallway. Or when I'm coming in for the meetings. He's always looking at the tourists with this—leering eye. And he has an erection.

NETTA: All the time? Always? He always has an erection?

GINA: That's hilarious.

VALESKA: Enough. Enough of the time. He has plenty of erections. That's all I'm saying. And I don't think it's hilarious. He could hurt someone. // His vibe. Is menacing. Like he could have a psychic break. And do something. Do something off the deep end.

GINA: With his erection?

KAREN: Yeah my friend Sharon's daughter. That kind of goes with what she was saying about him.

GINA: Your friend Sharon's daughter who worked at the pool said she was afraid that Tim might go off the deep end?

KAREN: Yeah. *(NOT GETTING IT)*

GINA: Forget it. No. Don't you think that's funny?

NETTA: Yeah I got it.

GINA: Not funny?

NETTA: It's a little funny. It's pretty funny.

GINA: Then why aren't you laughing?

NETTA: Because I'm concerned! Do you think I should say something? Do you think I should say something to someone?

GINA: To who? To whom will you say something, and what will you say?

VALESKA: To your boss. You can say to your boss The maintenance boy is a sex maniac and a pervert and he gets erections when he looks at the female visitors to the museum.

GINA'S CELL PHONE RINGS.

NETTA: Yeah. Yeah I could say that.

GINA: Hello? // Unh-hunh yes it is that's right.

NETTA: Except I think my boss is a sex maniac and a pervert too. And anyway, Tim's a good maintenance man.

VALESKA: He's hardly a man.

GINA: Hello? … Hello?

SHE GOT CUT OFF.

NETTA: He's very good with the glass Val. He's good at cleaning the glass. And he's careful with the fragile items. I don't think he's ever broken one single thing.

VALESKA: OK well I'm just saying. Don't come running to me when there is an incident of sexual misconduct and—

NETTA: OK Valeska. I promise I won't. I promise I won't come running to you when there is an incident of sexual misconduct.

VALESKA: Good.

SUDDENLY,
SHLOMY BARGES INTO THE SUPPORT GROUP MEETING.

SHLOMY: Hello ladies!

THE SONG "ATOMIC" BY BLONDIE COMES ON SUPERLOUD. IT PLAYS FOR ONE MINUTE AND FORTY SECONDS (UNTIL BLONDIE SINGS THE WORD "ATOMIC" FOR THE FIRST TIME). EVERYONE LOOKS AT SHLOMY. AND KATE. AND EACH OTHER.

FINALLY, FAST, LOUD, BIG:

KATE: What are you doing here?!

SHLOMY: I needed to see you.

KATE: But you just saw me this morning.

56

SHLOMY: I needed to see more of you.

KATE: This meeting is only for women, Shlomy. You can't come in here!

SHLOMY: Why? Why is this meeting only for women? Do you women think that you are the only women who need to talk about this sort of thing?

NETTA: Who is this person? Who are you?

KATE: This is Shlomy.

GINA: Obviously it's her boyfriend.

VALESKA: I don't think so.

KATE: He's my hairdresser.

VALESKA: Yes, that's what I thought.

KATE: What do you mean that's what you thought?

VALESKA: Because he's gay, no? Aren't you gay?

SHLOMY: That's a stereotype.

VALESKA: Maybe but—

KATE: He isn't gay.

VALESKA: Yes he is.

KATE: No he isn't.

VALESKA: Yes he is.

KATE: No he isn't!

VALESKA: I think that he is.

KATE: No he isn't!

VALESKA: I'm pretty sure // that he is.

KATE: No he isn't, Valeska, I had sex with him this morning!

NETTA: What?!

GINA: Told you.

SHLOMY: We didn't have sex.

KATE: Well we were naked.

SHLOMY: But we didn't have sex.

VALESKA: And why didn't you have sex if you were naked?

SHLOMY: Because I'm gay all right! And because Kate doesn't like it.

KATE: You're gay?!

SHLOMY: I didn't think you'd notice.

VALESKA: You were right.

KATE: I like to have sex. I think.

SHE DOES. SHE'S JUST A LITTLE CONFUSED BY ALL THIS.

SHLOMY: No you don't.

KATE: But you were my boyfriend! We were having an affair!

SHLOMY: That part was true.

NETTA: No, see, you're not allowed to have a boyfriend Katie.

MARGERIE: I thought you were having an affair with your handy man.

KATE: That part was a lie.

GINA: *(TO MARGERIE)* You knew? How did you know?

KATE: I told her.

MARGERIE: She told me.

NETTA: You wanna know what else was a lie?
             I don't have a sister!

                    A BIG, WEIRD SILENCE.

KAREN: *(QUIET)* I wish I had those Twizzlers.

                    *TIM COMES BACK WITH THE PLANT. HE SETS IT
                    RIGHT INSIDE THE DOOR. IT WAS A MISTAKE.
                    APPARENTLY HE MADE SOME KIND OF MISTAKE.*

TIM: *(TO NETTA)* I'm sorry I—
             I'm sorry.

                    NETTA SHAKES HER HEAD. IT'S OK.

                    TIM LEAVES.

                    GINA'S CELL PHONE RINGS AGAIN.

GINA: Hello?

MARGERIE: *(QUIETLY, IN A PRIVATE MOMENT WITH VALESKA)* I really like
             your shoes.

VALESKA: Thank you.

MARGERIE: Can I touch them?

VALESKA: Sure.

                    *MARGERIE GETS DOWN ON THE FLOOR AND TOUCHES OR
                    SORT OF PETS VALESKA'S SHOES, WHICH MAYBE HAVE
                    SOME FLUFFY FUR ON THEM OR SOMETHING AND ARE
                    VERY BEAUTIFUL AND UNUSUAL LIKE WORKS OF ART.*

GINA: Unh-hunh, yes.

MARGERIE: They're really great. Where did you get them?

VALESKA: My husband sent them to me once from … somewhere … I can't remember.

GINA: OK we'll be right over.

MARGERIE: He has really good taste.

VALESKA: I know.

GINA: We'll be right there.

VALESKA: Sweden!

GINA: That was Rebecca's neighbor's neighbor calling. Apparently Rebecca's not doing so good she thinks one of us should go over there.

REBECCA: Do you want to know
            what is in my mind, Horace?
            When I close my eyes for a long time? Do you want to know what I see?
            Nothing. There's nothing there.

NETTA: How does Rebecca's neighbor's neighbor know that Rebecca is not doing so good?

GINA: Said she saw her through a window. Apparently her windows are made of two-way glass. Said she wasn't looking over there for any particular reason, but who knows? Maybe this neighbor-neighbor is some kind of a spy.

NETTA: Well how'd she get your number? How'd she know to call you?

GINA: I don't know. I guess they had a conversation once. And she has a keen eye for a situation obviously. Some kind of a do-gooder I suppose. In any case, I think we should all go over there.

KATE: No! I'm not going over there! I can't go over there! You'll have to excuse me. Clearly, I have some thinking to do. I'm leaving. And I'm taking the Eiffel Tower with me.

KATE STORMS OUT WITH THE DONUTS.

KAREN: Sayonara.

BEAT. BEAT.

KAREN: That means good-bye.

NETTA: All right all right. Let's go. Let's go let's go let's go!

NETTA, MARGERIE, GINA, AND VALESKA GET INTO GINA'S SUV. KAREN STAYS BEHIND IN THE CONFERENCE ROOM WITH SHLOMY.

SHLOMY: Excuse me, are you Russian? Or German, or...?

KAREN: I'm American.

SHLOMY: Oh. Because you're wearing your ring on the right finger. I mean, on the wrong finger, on the right hand. I mean, on the wrong hand, on the right hand on the right finger. Are you married?

KAREN: Yes, but oh—No, this isn't mine. I mean. It falls off if I wear it on the other hand. My left hand is smaller than my right hand for some reason.

SHLOMY: Hm. And the foot as well?

KAREN: Yes the foot as well.

SHLOMY: And...?

KAREN: Yes everything. All of it. Bigger over there.

SHLOMY: Hunh. Also I notice that it is 18 karat, is that right?

KAREN: Uhm ... I think so. Yes. As I said, it isn't mine. I wanted
            rose gold. Do you know about that? It's kind of pink.

SHLOMY: Yes. So there are a lot of clues there.

VALESKA: (TO MARGERIE) This is the stage of the deployment
            which is characterized by feelings of excitement,
            denial, hunger, confusion, and euphoria.

MARGERIE: Should we talk about things that are possible but not
            likely?

                    VALESKA SHAKES HER HEAD NO.

KAREN: Did you ever have a boyfriend?

SHLOMY: I had one once but I wasn't that attracted to him.
            I think if he had developed into a completely different
            person, I could have spent the rest of my life with
            him.

KAREN: Or you. If you had developed into a completely different
            person.

SHLOMY: No. I don't think the completely different person I
            would have developed into would have found him
            attractive either. I think it would have had to have been
            him. He would have had to have done the different
            developing.

MARGERIE: I'm afraid my husband is going to leave me. Not the
            one I have, but the one I might have had.

VALESKA: Yes he might. It's a strong possibility.

HORACE: Do you have anything that might cheer us up?

REBECCA: I don't think so. Oh, oh! Oh, no. I gave it away.
            You want another band-aid?

HORACE: Can I get some water?

REBECCA: In the kitchen.

HORACE EXITS.

KAREN: You can come home with me. If you want.

SINCE OBVIOUSLY HE ISN'T GOING HOME WITH KATE.

SHLOMY: I don't think that's appropriate Karen. Maybe in three months' time it will be OK. But today, I don't think it's right.

THE LADIES ARRIVE SUDDENLY IN REBECCA'S BATHROOM.

REBECCA: What is this? What is this is this an intervention?

NETTA: We don't know. We just came over.

GINA: We wanted to see you. See how you were.

REBECCA: Were?

GINA: Are.

REBECCA: *(TO MARGERIE)* Who are you?

MARGERIE: I'm Margerie.

NETTA: This is the new girl.

REBECCA: Nice to meet you.

MARGERIE: Nice to meet you too.

KAREN: I have been to Siberia, Shlomy. And they have motorcycles there. And juke boxes. And snow. Do you want to go there with me? We can go there and have a beer and we can forget all about it.

SHLOMY: Maybe in three months' time.

KAREN: Or tomorrow! If you come tomorrow, I will bring you
                something nice.

SHLOMY: I appreciate it. Really I do but for now, I would rather if
                you could—Forgive me but … let me be.

REBECCA: Do you want something? Something to drink or
                something?

NETTA: No, that's OK.

GINA: I do.

REBECCA: Is water OK?

GINA: Yeah that's great.

REBECCA LEAVES.
NETTA GIVES GINA A LONG LOOK.

GINA: What? I'm thirsty.

NETTA: Do you ever stop thinking about yourself Gina?

GINA: No. Do you?

NETTA: I try.

GINA: But do you succeed? Do you?

NETTA:

GINA: No. Because you can't stop thinking about yourself.
                Not for one minute. Or else you'll get attacked.
                Viscously attacked. Immediately // the moment you—

NETTA: Viciously?

GINA: Yes.

NETTA: Viciously attacked?

GINA: Yes!

NETTA: Because you said viscously. You said viscously attacked which would mean—

GINA: No I didn't, I did?

VALESKA: Yeah. You did.

NETTA: *(GOING ON)* I don't even know what that would mean. I can't even begin to imagine what that would mean!

MARGERIE: That would be some kind of a slow, thick...

GINA: This is off the point! This is not why we're here!

KAREN: Is it three months' time yet? Will you come home with me now or go to Siberia or some suburb? I think it would make me happy. And I can see that you have nothing better to do. Although you think that you have important—concerns.

REBECCA AND HORACE COME BACK WITH GLASSES OF WATER.

REBECCA: Here you go.

GINA: Now who are you?

REBECCA: Who are you talking to?

GINA: Him!

VALESKA: That is probably *her* boyfriend.

REBECCA: You can see him?

GINA: What do you mean I can see him?

NETTA: Sweetie, he's right there.

REBECCA: *(YIKES!)* He is?

GINA: Uhm, yeah.

VALESKA: Wow this is really bad hunh?

REBECCA: Horace?

HORACE: Yes?

> *LITTLE PAUSE.*

REBECCA: You're real?

HORACE: *(SHRUGS)*

> *LITTLE PAUSE.*

NETTA: Wait a minute. I know you. You're that guy. You're a
            Civil War reenactor. You're a Civil War reenactor! I've
            seen you in the parades.

REBECCA: Is that true, Horace?

HORACE: Somewhat.

REBECCA: You're not Horace Hunley?

GINA: Ah Jesus.

HORACE: I play him in the parades.

> *LITTLE PAUSE.*

REBECCA: What do you do in real life?

HORACE: I'm your neighbor.

> *LITTLE PAUSE.*

REBECCA: What's your name?

HORACE: Gary.

REBECCA: Like the city? Like the town in Indiana?

HORACE: Yeah.

PAUSE.

REBECCA: I think you should go now, Gary. I want to thank you for stopping by and all that you did but—I think you should go now. OK?

GARY: OK but. You be careful Rebecca. These walls they're paper thin you know?

REBECCA: I know. These walls they are paper thin.

A LONG STILLNESS WHILE GARY DOESN'T LEAVE.

GARY: All right well. You take care Rebecca.

REBECCA: You too Gary.

HE STILL DOESN'T LEAVE.
THEY LOOK AT EACH OTHER.

GARY DRINKS THE WHOLE GLASS OF WATER, HANDS
THE EMPTY GLASS TO REBECCA, AND LEAVES.

NETTA: Oh my god!

GINA: Are you OK?

REBECCA: Yeah. I'm OK. I think so. What happened?

GINA: Apparently your neighbor Gary broke into your house and spent the day with you in your bathroom.

REBECCA: Someone tell me their life story. Quick. In three words and an object.

MARGERIE: Dog bite.

VALESKA: Champs-Elysée.

NETTA: Housekeeper.

GINA: Kitschy lamp.

REBECCA: *(TO GINA)* Somewhere, there is documentation of the
                two of us having a conversation where I asked you to
                look into my eyes and tell me what you saw there.

GINA: What did I say?

REBECCA: You said I looked fine.

GINA: And what did you say?

REBECCA: I said: I simply don't see how that is possible.

GINA: Damn it Rebecca! A lot of people don't get what
                they want out of life. A lot of young people dream
                of adventure, travel, success, wealth, luxury, and it
                doesn't happen. They stay in the same small town
                they're in and they have smaller lives than that. But it's
                OK. It's oh-kay.

                        *MEANWHILE, KATE HAS COME BACK INTO THE
                        CONFERENCE ROOM TO CONFRONT SHLOMY.*

KATE: I don't know why you did this, but I think the only reason
                you did this is to distract yourself from the abyss of
                meaninglessness that is under your feet. Since that is
                why I did it too, I suppose I would like to find a way for
                us to forgive each other, Shlomy.

SHLOMY: I'd like that.

KAREN: So I guess you really don't want to come home with
                me after all. Is that what I'm to understand?

SHLOMY: *(TO KAREN)* I think I owe you an apology.

MARGERIE: I think we all owe everyone an apology. I think every
                single one of us owes every single person we've ever
                met an apology.

ALL: I don't know what to tell you.
I'm sorry?
What's good enough?
Is that good enough?
I'm sorry.
You look at me like that.
I could look at you like that too.
You think I want to be here? In this position? I don't.
Believe me when I tell you that I don't.

I don't know. It's true. And you don't know either. So
what, so you think I should be punished? Oh I'm being
punished all right. Yes I am. Right now. Doing this?
Right now? I'm suffering. And I think—I could be wrong
but—no—yeah—I'm pretty sure you're suffering too.
I think that's what I can see there. On your face. Yep.
Pretty sure that looks like suffering. And pretty sure I
know what it looks like. It's like looking in a mirror.

OK but yes. I'm doing it again. I'm talking about you.
I'm telling you what you think, telling you what you feel,
I'm thinking about you. They tell me that's my beautiful
plan. I mean my—habitual pattern. They say I'd rather
look out
than look in.
I say, Who wouldn't?
Because sure
if you can think about all that, out there
(and there's plenty of it out there to think about)
I say, If you can think about all that then
why think about all this instead?
If you can think about all that then
you don't have to think about what is.
And who wants to think about what is?
I don't.
I'd rather think about you and what I think are your
problems.
Or how nice it would be to
go on a holiday with you and
get a lemon ice and
have sex with you in a public place.

Yeah. I could think about that all day.

Would much rather think about that than

well just about anything really.

*MARGERIE APPROACHES THE AUDIENCE. SHE HANDS
OUT LITTLE WALLET-SIZED PICTURES OF HER
HUSBAND TO SEVERAL PEOPLE. HER HUSBAND IS
WEARING A NAVY UNIFORM IN THE PICTURE.*

MARGERIE: It was his arms. In the end. That were everything.
On that first spring day. On that first spring day when
he came in in short sleeves. I saw that he had a
tattoo. On his left forearm. Here. It said: Diabetique.
Diabetique.
Everyone is so fragile. We got married that following
June.

REBECCA: Dear Horace Hunley,
I realize that you are not my uncle.
That you are not my father.
That you are not alive,
and I am.

I don't feel I know myself any better,
though I seem to have
gotten through the day.

You appeared here
and were gone.
The same will be true of me I suppose
one day.

Please give everyone my regards.
When you see them. My regrets.
Tell them I said hello.
Tell them I'm sorry.
Tell them I'm not Linda.
Tell them I'm working on it.

KAREN: When you are first learning Japanese
they teach you to say things like

Where is the tree? and
The tree is in the garden.

Where is the tree.
As though, when you arrive, you might suddenly
find yourself
in need of a tree
or as though
you might suddenly have lost the one
you had come to rely on
to keep your bearings
or whatever.

Where is the tree.

The tree is in the garden.

E N D   O F   P L A Y

Conceive of the text
as material for labor,
for the work of production.

— WB Worthen

NOTES ON THE PLAY

PRODUCTION

While my personal visual aesthetic tends toward the minimal, which is suggested in this script, it is not my intention to limit the potential or diminish the importance of the design element. On the contrary, the design (whether sparse or dense) should take an equally strong position on the stage as the actors, text, and direction. I would only like to suggest that the design need not reiterate what is made clear by the language, and/or the behavior of the actors.

SCRIPT/NARRATIVE/CHARACTERS

While at first glance this script might resemble a traditional play (with characters who have names, relationships, back stories), it is not intended to function as a literary drama. It is a text for speaking. The narrative or story elements of the play are there to be enjoyed as such, but they are also intentionally fleeting, unstable, and non-culminating.

There are errors of speech and logic in the play. Best not to dwell on them.

Look for the play in how it moves and sounds more than in what it says. A similar approach should be applied to the characters.

Speaking of the characters, it is important that the women are friends. They like each other. They are not miserable, crazy, or mean.

notes

HELLO FAILURE BY KRISTEN KOSMAS
One thousand copies of this first edition
were printed and bound in the autumn of
2009 by MᶜNAUGHTON & GUNN in the
state of Michigan, near the Saline River,
using 100% recycled FSC certified paper.
The covers were printed offset on Tiziano
paper by POLYPRINT DESIGN on the
shores of the Hudson River in New York City,
and letterpressed at the UGLY DUCKLING
PRESSE workshop on the Gowanus Canal
in Brooklyn, New York. Design by DON'T
LOOK NOW! Typeset in Akzidenz Gothic,
Orator, and Bulmer.

KRISTEN KOSMAS is a playwright and
performer. She has had plays commissioned
by Performance Space 122, Seattle
University's SITE Specific, Dixon Place,
and New City Theater. Her plays include
THIS FROM CLOUDLAND, HELLO
FAILURE, CHAPTER OF ACCIDENTS,
THE MAYOR OF BALTIMORE, ANTHEM,
and PALOMINO. She is the writer and
performer of four critically acclaimed solo
shows, THE SCANDAL!, SLIP, AGAIN,
and BLAH BLAH FUCKIN BLAH, which
have been performed at venues in New
York, Austin, Boston, Seattle, and Chicago.
Texts forthcoming include THIS FROM
CLOUDLAND (Play A Journal of Plays),
and THE MAYOR OF BALTIMORE AND
ANTHEM (53rd State Press).

EMERGENCY PLAYSCRIPTS promotes
texts which, through their performance, can
expand the practice of theater. The series
is edited and published by Auguste & Louis
Lumière for UGLY DUCKLING PRESSE.